MAIDEN

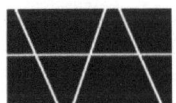

Maiden ©**2020** *by* **Travis Tate.** Published in the United States by Vegetarian Alcoholic Press. Not one part of this work may be reproduced without expressed written consent from the author. For more information please contact vegalpress@gmail.com

Cover art by Jasmine Choi

I.
RELIGION   3
ON BEING RECKLESS   4
SOMETIMES YOU ARE FAUNA, SOMETIMES YOU ARE A BELL   5
IN CAGED SMOKE   9
FOR THE GARDEN WE'LL SHARE   10
THE HORSE   11
MOTH   13
ABLUTION   14

II.
FIRST LETTER TO DAVID   19
ON WANTING TO BE LOVED   20
THIS (UN)HOLY DESIRE   22
TO M.   23
WHEN I FEEL DEATH CLOSE   24
OPAL   26
ODE   28
WHAT THE NIGHT DOES   29

III.
SECOND LETTER TO DAVID   33
ASPIRATIONS   34
BOOK OF REVELATION   35
DRAGON   36
MOTHER DRIVES TO ARIZONA   38
WHICH PARADISE ARE YOU TALKING ABOUT?   39
GABRIEL, HANIEL, ARIEL   40
JACOB   41
FIRST LOVE   46
LOST FLOWER   47

IV.
DREAM OF MEADOWLARKS   51
THE SECOND COMING OF MARY   52
MICHELANGELO   53
ON ADDICTION   54
WHAT HAPPENS AT DAWN   57
NON BINARY   58
ON LOSING YOUR MEMORY (DEMENTIA)   59
WHAT IT FEELS LIKE AT THE END   60
WHEN YOU ARE READY TO LOVE AGAIN   62
PSALMS   63

"To burn with desire and keep quiet about it is the greatest punishment we can bring on ourselves."
-*Federico Garcia Lorca*

I.

RELIGION

I'm starting a new religion.
We only worship things that are green.

Each morning, we take a pill. Each night, we take
another. We say snappy things, quips, impressions.

Sayings we'll know will dig. But we always wait
for a smile. That's a rule. Always wait for a smile.

The danger of failing is required holy text. Here,
the soft dim of sunset is praise. Scripture tells us

to strain the neck forward while the body stands
still. We will worship your hand accidently touching

my knee. How holy is the soft touch of the one you
love. & the one who loves you. Don't forget to pray.

Say *O small grape. O ballast heart. We believe in you.*
& we will feel better. Not worshipping the same bleached

knees. Isn't life grand? I know- I hate to think that too.
But look at birds. & the roaches. Aren't they weird? They

worship nothing at all. I think reincarnation is nice.
We were all birds once. Now we can worship each

person's hands in their pockets. I want today &
tomorrow to not catch me in the same way. To make

me over each mooning. Hope is eternal longing. Faith is
a garbage bag, no matter how overstuffed, won't break.

ON BEING RECKLESS

have an appetite for your uncut mouth
   limping towards what looks like your face

there, in a light sage cloud,
desire is not minimal, unleashed by

not sucking down the same pill every day.

when giving in wins, it's 3 a.m
& nothing happens.

the light of desire remains
   until what is satisfied within the gut

or the mind, or the wind between lungs & brain

is finally crushed like a small petaled flower under a boot

until we are fishing things out of each other

everything here is dying,

   even my love for you.

SOMETIMES YOU ARE FAUNA, SOMETIMES YOU ARE A BELL

1.

Omission of a thing allows it to grow.
If you keep it taped down, it finds a way

to creep up the underside of old toys
left in the lawn. I admit you do look rusty.

I cannot love you for any more of the time
that we're going to be left here,

    sweetness.

2.

David is the devil in bed. David,
the bed warmer, is gone. Is only

breathing closely to glass. David
is warm air & thick mist.

3.

Wreath of quiet Friday night.

4.

Silly little closet of grief,
hides its weight in the liver.
I stand where you stand. I

bleed where you bleed. Great
permanent seizure. Unhook

your mouth from me. I'm still
bleeding draped over your
invisible back in the weighted

evenings.

IN CAGED SMOKE

in the middle of nowhere bright birds.
cats roam bamboo.   night stalkers.
leaves of metal & chairs. we hope you can be there.
you're always invited to sit near the ground
soaking up: beer   dust   & carcinogens.
tomorrow the bedroom. next your house. next:
anything.
even if the air is saccharine   your kiss
much sweeter your laugh   much sweeter.
time will fall away. we'll be stuck here forever.
& i'm okay with that.

FOR THE GARDEN WE'LL SHARE

"Green, how I desire you, green."
-Federico Garcia Lorca

The garden is green, muted tones of lilac.
I hold your hands. Then I hold your ribs.
Back & forth, we rock. The garden is

green maleficent lips. Back & forth, we,
sea-blue, your lips, large ship, kiss me.
It will be our common tongue of

brotherhood. In the garden, you have
hair. Because I do not. Something for me
to play with. In the garden, we are brown.

The garden is green-
No, emerald.

Our bodies entwined with rope. The cool
rain filling up the earth near our knees,
your hands between my thighs. I love

you. The cool rain is a reminder,
like some simple tool of god.

The garden is our prize.

THE HORSE

We are destined to think of father
riding home, briskly, on his favorite
horse. The delicate black mane.
The wind blowing against his thin jaw.

While father is on his way home,
we are blue-lipped & thinking
of the man one day we'll truly love.

We are not bothered by
the many messages about
the darkness of our skin.

The horse is brown,
sometimes black,
we think.
& shut our eyes for a moment
to be strong thighed
& moving on four legs.

While father, on his way home,
almost breathless, being
whipped by the bridle wind,
we are cleaning out boxes
of memories & the hung bells
are ringing six o'clock.

No one is set out to
love us,
they say.

It is always a miscalculation on their part. We are often
thrown in the trash, a broken-legged equus,
no longer able to run & leap in the air for them.

We never get to love.
We, a blanket lit afire
to keep them warm.

Father is sweeping over tall grass,
his ankles, a fast-paced forestry.

MOTH

I thought in the darkness
look at those fat ass moths.

Light sweeping through their
brown skin. Love for a thing

that is unlike you is common.
Flying towards & away from

grace. To be the thing unlike
what your brain regulates.

& always, forever, reaching.

ABLUTION

I started washing my hands more often,
ablution near breakfast, slow tea. & funny,
there are no red-winged birds greeting
my unbrushed teeth. I'm always looking for signs
in the cosmic. I have to learn to love the bridge
of uncertainty, its wobble & crude craftsmanship.
I turn my face up to look in the mirror. There,
a crooked-faced bird. In my eyes. Latched to my face.

I have learned that often I do not say aloud the things
I want in fear of doing it wrong. My therapist, who is
also gay, who also sweats a lot, gave me papers with
things to say to myself when those rapid thoughts
crotch down under my tongue. Is therapy a kind of
ablution? When I'm done in the mirror, there is
no magic.

I'm desperate to fix the body. Stop watching
it squirm in the mirror. I could throw away
all the clothes & shoes underneath the bed.
Start painting my nails, wearing flowery
long shirts that remind me of my mother.

My mother says the devil is working against us.

Everyone is so afraid of the devil. I let him into
my mouth, into the bare back. Let the devil
into my dreams, floating mast of horns.
This body is grateful for a small while, grateful
for the cliffs ahead on the long ride home.

When I look out the window,
a fawn, grazing close to the grass,
its wet nose steaming.

The cruel winter is just a season.

II.

FIRST LETTER TO DAVID

David, some people have bad tattoos.
Below the ankle. Round of the cheek.

Something about permanence. The body must
be reckoned with. Sharp shoulders.

At 18,
I told you this-
I got my first tattoo. Snake with skull.
Villian from my favorite childhood book.

Scars, David, are small reminders.
Like the wrist is for the arm and hand.

I want to be something I'm not sure I will become.

There is a way to write the future.
Scent of uncombed hair, that lavender.

Stars are aligning, David.
In the distance, fog & the belly of a mountain.

ON WANTING TO BE LOVED

Moments before I arrived here to you,
I was sleeping. On my back. Face to the
ceiling of my crooked apartment. Your eyes

have this thing. I'm not sure what it is. It looks
like you may be wearing eyeliner. Here I go again, falling
in love with anyone I meet.

It's curious.

I played this game earlier this week.
It was called "imaginary bf." & I'm quite good at it.

First, you think of the name of
a pretend boyfriend. It has
to be a good name. A name you want
to look at when
light is creeping across his face.
Moon. Or Sun. Or glow of a camera.

Then, you make up scenarios where it would be hard to love
him. But in the end, you decide to love him.

This conversation is always to a friend.

After this, you must imagine his greeting.
His usual one. For you.

When that feeling right
above the pelvis hits.

He meets your friends.
What does he say?
All good things.
All the right things.

You dream up two kids.
Papa. Baba. Dad. Paws.

All the names they'll call
to you when you're no
doubt sleeping.

He dies before you do.
& you mourn him.
You think of heaven
for the first time
in 35 years.

THIS (UN)HOLY DESIRE

I desire your holy wishes.

Sweat pressing through the back
of your shirt.

Holy dove soap. Holy
        wine. Jesus, his sceptre & Mary

Magdalene smiling because she knows
she never wept at his feet.
        It was the other way around.

I desire your teeth in my chest.
        Your nails in the headboard.
Your pulsing, arched back.

After
        I imagine what you would
look like as an angel.

& what wings. & what body.
& the light.

TO M.

My mother says that the accounting class
at the local community college
is too hard for her. & I know what she means.

She means
the glass eye that is watching her
is gleaming & spinning & splitting open.

She means
too hard
in the way
the river
at her feet
is exceedingly
drying out
everyday.

I say

  I am a river

My mother says
she is now moving
to Arizona
with her mother.

The cancer-riddle kidney will stay in Texas.
& the oncoming dementia will follow.

The maternal line is always tipping.

My mother says
she is often anxious,
reflects in the mirror
a face she does not want,
carries around the bodies
of the one's she loves.

And I say
  Me too, mom, mommy, mum, mummy, ma, ma, m, m

WHERE I FEEL DEATH CLOSE

Every year I get older,
the mind breaks like

winter into spring. Today,
I feel like washing away

my genitals & calling my
mother to say goodbye.

Being a faggot, who calls
on ghosts

to commune with
in slow moments, is a hard

existence. Being a black faggot-
wonder how the mind is broken like this-

wonder of

a world where you
are unafraid of me

& I give you a slick lily.

My father found the gay porn
I printed out on our home
computer. He took me on

a car ride to tell me

*you can't be gay
& black*

So I listened to him
like a bible. His words,
like fists, like blades.

Often, I forget.
The rose on the window sill,
all dried up.

I forget that even with all the drugs
that everyday I'm reborn to myself .

Yesterday, I read a Sylvia Plath
poem. & thought
the mirror, a prism of light,
reflecting what was already gone,
was untruthful.

Faggot's eye-
that sleep hooks in
like the dark skin
around the trunk
of a tree.

Then I woke today
& felt the same way,
felt sheer dynamite-

something like a smokescreen
of contentment-

God, Jehovah-

made my body this hole,
this deep-

I want my body to unhinge-
come back together like what
it really wants to be-

dangerous.
Or, loved.

OPAL

Those raincoats
are not needed.
Leave them
over the back of the couch.

Pebbles
the size of stones
wade over
the opal sky.

We are hiding
in this parking garage.

We've kissed
twice today
in hidden places.

Once here, now.
The other in a soft dream.

I hate the hands
that my grandmother gave me.
I seek out yours
in this parking garage.

& the sky opens up like
a well sliced mango.

Then you breach
my welded insides,
you slice me open.
Dark body, a grave.

You are constantly
standing over me.

I have not trusted
the word "man"
for so long.

Opal earrings
in a drawer
near the sink,
next to
some other boy's
bloodied hands
I stole.

The sound of pebbles overhead.

We'll be stuck here forever.

I am the sky.
Opal,
dead thing,
right above you.

ODE

like a sad song.
terrapin alone in a marshy green.

gossamer.
what name is that for my hands?

O. Joy.
I will always love you.

words are desperate, always in the air, singing.
smooth stone pressed into my clavicle.

sinner.
save me jesus.

blackened ankles. bones hold boxes
of small coins shaped like souls.

meaty gems spread on bread.
eat me.

O. Lavender.

look at my fat wrist.
bushy groves that cover his arms.

I have nothing. If I don't have you.

WHAT THE NIGHT DOES

The cat's paw, the hill on which stones lay dead,
the beaten macaw, cracked beak-
they all ring to me in the modest October nights.

I shouldn't talk about night like a spell.

What comes to me like quaking?

The lips of a boy. The starling,
some new prince of the universe,
a heart split in two by a hatchet.

I'm always willing to say I am fine while I'm burning.

I'm having the same conversations with myself, resting my head on a gun.

The gossamer dahlias
that are resembling the lighted nightsky,
I'm asking them to kill me.

I am a demon, charging myself, in the night.
Pressed against myself, I breath in.
& suddenly a merry-go-round of blackbirds.
They are my graces.

In Night, I undo the smallness of my approach.
I do not blink the eyes,
dark orbs inhaling what brings them joy.

III.

SECOND LETTER TO DAVID

Before or after Isaac? Son as onus?
Isaac didn't know his father was a murderer.

I digress, David.

You don't care if the picture in the mirror is fading. Look,
how old the roses at the foot of the bed have gotten. Chrysalis,
color of where your legs meet your pelvis. David, would you

move to New York? We don't have to live in the city- just off
the Hudson River. There's trash on the curb. I could watch you
from the stoop as you walk back from the market. A single thread

of light. From your hips. Your shirt half untucked. Crooked smile.
I can feel my skull shifting apart like some animal's skull, floating
to the surface of salty water. But you put your lips near my lungs,

David. A body is a body is yours is my body.

ASPIRATIONS

I want to be good at one thing. & it not be
conversing with the devil. I want it to
be good at eating healthy food. & not smoking

cigarettes every evening until my eyes
close around the world. I want to be
good at the way to say goodbye

& mean it. There is a bit of strength
needed in being talented. & well,
the talent part too. I want goodness
to be one of my main attributes.

Maybe one day be smart enough
to understand politics. Or maybe,
be so good at being happy I never

know what clouds form above my head
every day. The devil is smiling
somewhere, yellow grin. I want to

be the word *lost* for a while then
find myself in a garden, where I'm
spinning & pollen is poking my nose.

I'm bad at saving money. Or asking
for help. I'm bad at being alone. I'm
bad for you. & for him too. I'm bad
at keeping the house clean & going

to bed at a decent hour. I'm bad at
loving myself. I'm bad at writing.

What's good
about being bad
is you have to learn
to be good.

BOOK OF REVELATION

I ate a tangelo, a small citrus fruit, & mary magdalene cries in the evening.
I ate your tongue, grilled, & tonight, I'll braid your black hair.

I will always pale in comparison to mary. I know. I won't make it to
apostle. I want your cocoa buttered hands. Only to remind me of my own body.
Like mary did for jesus, reminded him of his feet & the long journey ahead.

I ate the pit of a peach, the rind of a watermelon, the seeds of a jackfruit.

I want you black boy
& I want to unearth a body that looks like mine (my own body)
every morning to the light.
But we are not allowed to have each other.

I ate the pills this morning,
white, white, yellow, triangle, circle. & now the funny thing is
I want more pills.

I ask *what is the sin of the world?*

The pills call down the seven spirits of g-d.
When I take my pills, the sky recedes like a scroll & all the stars

fall from heaven to earth, where I stand & wait for you,
my brother. My home. My revelation.

DRAGON

i.

i'm on my knees,
        and the thunder hits.

ii.

i'm crying into my hands, using the tears
        to wash red pears at moonlight. i desire
the brief longing on a man.

the way my feet are making a V,
                              the flight of blackbirds.

iii.

all the nightingales stop singing.

iv.

i am lonely
        like a black-knife.

v.

i am so tired of being a black boi.

vi.

my ears, the cool cracking neck, the wallows of my hands.
they feel abundant, they weigh down the rest of the body.

vii.

one day, i'll be so preciously martyred, so many broken arrows
        through the chest. i just want to be held by a pond,
        a golden fish in your eye.

i want the whole world.
        & you, slayed.

MOTHER DRIVES TO ARIZONA

Watching your mother grow
is an enlightening endeavor.

Watching flowers bloom from
her forehead like a newly

pruned garden. The world
is so unfair. But she makes

everything pleasant. Butterfly.
You watch her as her mother

dies & think how it will be
replaced. The garden is

shrinking. Soon you'll have
sprouts of your own. Tending

to them when the cool air
is breaking light over their

faces. But for now,
you drive this dark highway

alone.

WHICH PARADISE ARE YOU TALKING ABOUT?

Mention paradise
& forget you're dying.

There is pleasure in
undeniable blood

that pull like great fish
on a thin line. Mothers

begat mothers
here in this state

of wildflowers. Blackness
is sitting in silence,

a roach on a wooden floor.
Where can you go if you

are damned? It rains. It gets
colder & sharp air

fills your lungs. Gifts
are placed on an altar

for everyone who has
ever lost any thing

or any body. Paradise
is weeping for all of you.

GABRIEL, HANIEL, ARIEL

You deserve angels. You're owed golden.
You & the pedestal you're waiting to

sit on. You've lost everything stable.
Watching the sun catch the sky

purple so early. You are waiting in line
for another grandmother to die. Only

thing you can do is flower at your own
grave. Here, the diamonds are being

made. & you being washed in-
for a third time by those who are fallen,

gracious paradise awaits you, simply, one day.
You are looking for love. To replace

what's lost inside of you. Night blooms
a small breeze. You are light air

filled with the scent of lavender. You are
not cursed like you think you are. Grace

is a burden you must discover in your own.
You will get what you want. Charging stones

in midnight light. You will be the thing you
want. One day. You are holding on. You don't

stop. You don't kill yourself. You are dancing.
You are music. You are beauty

like silk trees pressed with dew. Night
falling. The music is playing

from somewhere far off and is still
audible. You are future redwoods.
Bold, tall. & growing as you die.

JACOB

*

He is wrestling the angel
at a riverbank. His family has
crossed the river already.

      & he is left alone.

Jacob goes all night
        with the Angel of the Lord.

Meaning, Jacob is battling with
a more powerful thing than himself.

This happens at the beginning of the Bible.
Just to set the tone, I suppose.

*

After, essentially, wrestling with God all night,
a torn hip from his socket, Jacob commands

    a blessing for himself.

*

I think about this for rest of the day-
there is discussion about whether
Jacob is just wrestling a man. Or if,
in fact, he is wrestling God. Or just
some ordinary angel. See, there's a
confusion with the translation. It's
either "an" or "the." In other sections
of the bible, it's believed that certain
angels embody God. & for those who
see the angel, it is like they are,
as Jacob puts it,   "face to face with God."

*

What if I'm not where I'm supposed to be?
What angel?
What match of strength?
Is this my hip ripping from its socket,
sinew on thigh?

Question what made us. Question
the light. Question what Abraham
gives to his children. Question how
strong I am. How strong I'll have
to be. Clearly, the night seeps in,
water on your skin, reflective, clean.

*

The angel gives Jacob a new name.
    The angel blesses Jacob.

FIRST LOVE

The night contains
a light, fissure, atomic.
I only know that's true
because of the drinking.

That's what it's doing,
quelling the insufficient.
No one is asking me
to bear the weight of

the sun. A picture like,
like some Greek myth.
I wanted your light.
Untameable Texas sun.

Even when behind
a night curtain, it tills
the skin. Makes you
desirable. Even when

I take the time to
dream up new love,
new boyfriends, cute
& sweet, enchanting.

The night fissures,
fusion of your
pierced nipples.
When I was in

high school, I said
*You can love someone
you don't even know.*
& the sky is above of us.

LOST FLOWER

He doesn't want to taste the basil of your lips. Garden the mound
of dirt you claim to be. He's made of thick roots, like you. Especially,

in the autumn, the blooming is ripe. The fruit of your legs & arms,
the fuzzy peach of your cheek. He's often a slow watered creek,

blistering towards you. He hasn't found you yet. He's making
his way to you, stream, over a boulder, swan's song. The sky

above is singing. It is always singing. How soft, a ting, light rain.
Thank god, it is the last summer. You open your mouth. Wait

for the rain. His mouth, too, is waiting to open. He wants to do
that flirty voice, pearled in roses. Look at you with the eyes

of a deadly rattlesnake. Bend over some great field you're always in,
smell the tip, just the edge of you. How glorious it is to be a beautiful scent,

be washed by god every evening. How glorious, the pane of moon
on your brow. You are a simple boy, constantly wanting to be covered

in chrysanthemum ink. The deluge of lust always hits in the waking
black of night. Touching your face & limp crotch. You are made

to flower here longer. He is meant for echoes. He is not meant for grace.

IV.

DREAM OF MEADOWLARKS

of some man laying his head in your left armpit

dream of

of your grandmother's noodle soup

she can no longer make

of her lifting her arms to say goodbye

of the duality of wanting something

& knowing it's not a good thing for you

dream dream dream

of wet november

of what brought you to this edge in the first place

& what brings you back to your own bed every evening

dream of sleeping

of everything already in its rightful place

THE SECOND COMING OF MARY

You are lost, no -
You are softening the tender stretch of my neck.

I'm able to breathe quick, running circles around my father.
His grief unspeakable.

He hangs his head,
dying flower of Indiana.

The body is gone.

But the shape of gravity is known. We carry her,
like a folded jacket of spirit, laying in our arms.

I ask John The Baptist, *what is the sound of coming*.
& he replies, *breaking air*.

The angel Gabriel, coasting down on thunder,
making lightning for the first time in the world.

Her name, *Mary*, hangs,
dead flower of Indiana.

My father & I don't say her name.
We let the air do it, breaking,
lightning upon our heads.

MICHAELANGELO

It's seemingly beautiful, the curved hand made
of stone. The three dots before you respond to
my clever joke. Sometimes beauty is wanting
what other people have. I understand that
jealousy is greenish but envy is pink. The skin

between David's thumb & pointer finger. The
broken clock on the wall. I'm watching people
leave. Some for good. & some just for a time.

My heart aches the same.
My body reshuffles itself.

In 1991, a "deranged man" hit David on the foot,
with a hammer, changing the marble. Maybe he
was trying to reform what we think of the modern
ideal man. Or, maybe, he was aware that everything
must & will change. I'll be unkind to myself if I watch

your shadows.

I want change. I've been craving it. But for some
reason or other, I can't make myself do it. I should
at least dip my toe in. Or should I wait until
I can jump in, full body wet. I'm so confused.

One day, I will be David. Beat Goliath.

What makes beauty?
Is it longing?
Or you, bathed in light?

ON ADDICTION

Every evening, like prayers
to my goddess, I drink.

When day is cracked upon
my head, I say *tonight*

will be different. It is strange
the patterns we keep.

As a result, they become
a part of our personalities.

How I create myself
for you, is how I want

the angels to see me.
How I want my love

to see me. Broken, yet un-
tarnished. I deny myself

the pleasure of a reprieve-
Instead, douse the fire.

I lick my lips. I'm not
relaxed until I remember

your name in all its
low watt haunting. A current

runs like a saddled horse-
infinitely charged but tame.

There are still ghosts in
my loins & they ask to be fed

sweet juice, slowly, for hours
on end. Luck doesn't suddenly

make you into something else.
Neither does wanting a thing.

I think maybe then,
perseverance

but that's a trick too.
People do always ask

how did you get here?
& I cry because

I don't know how I got here.

Which makes me think
I'm tougher than I really am.

Or is it,

each day, I see my brain
chip away like old paint.

Watch my mother get older.
I want to reason with myself

or make some compromise
for my addiction-

if you watch three bells ring today-
if you are three bells ringing-

I never keep any promise. I'm late
to the parade of loving yourself.

I have trouble getting on. What's
delightful is that I haven't got

much more to give to you, prince.
If I were faster,

I would have learned quicker
to love you the right way.

The origin-
how'd you get here?

I'm guessing it could be
bloodshot DNA.

Could be societal
& systemic pressures.

But there's nowhere for
politics to stand in addiction.

Weep for your betterment,
even when disaster stays

helmed to the skirt
I wear in my fantasies.

What getting drunk really does,
every night for three years,

is makes you a flawless animal
in some jungle you've never seen

but know well from a TV program.
Makes you happy for a second

even if it leaves your bones ripped
from their sockets like so much

roadkill. I bleed
in the evening,

not red,
lilac.

WHAT HAPPENS AT DAWN

It's a wonder how you made it to this place -
its crimson gates, shelled by a tall choir.

You are bandaged.

The kindling has changed the fire from red
to the color of a blue jay, speckled with devil's snare.

The stretchmarks on your stomach
are from too much bringing your hand to your mouth.

You pulled your body -
one you didn't want -
from a grave each morning.

Now, all the trees bend, darkness creeps in a bit sooner,

you're married to the sea that keeps growing
inside your head, starlings part in anticipation.

NON BINARY

I'm beautiful when
I am stained

I think. This is the kind of

dance I'll do to make you love me. I haven't
had a crush on someone who I deem important
in so many years. Is this the taste of salt?
The way the body works-

the way MY works is the base on the rejection
of norms. Which is sad. The water is cold.
I already know it. Washing your feet
is biblical. Lot's wife. The garden. Hail,
the beauty of a body, torn. I walk away from the river.
Back to my body, for a few hours of-

ON LOSING YOUR MEMORY (DEMENTIA)

The fog, eating almost everything that is visible this morning, makes it feel
like living in a new place, a weird town. I realize as I drive far too fast
for the weather conditions, that I'm not very brave. It's unfortunate that,
as I'm careening through this wall of smoke, I'm so afraid of change.

It will be unlikely that I will ever gain any courage at all. I'll be stuck
down in this plain old body. Forever. Which is fine, I guess. To be
my own god. Reign this body for 89 years. I think when you get older
you move closer to your divinity. This is often why the mind tries to

erase itself. The body gives way to what light it seeks. & the knowledge
of this light is only known when the body is cresting between
worlds, planes, like half a body in water & the other half floating on
the horizon. I'll eventually have to leave this place even if there's

no money in the bank. & even though I hate traveling from my bed,
if I want to see the world, I'll have to learn to like it. I don't want
to love again. Not deeply. Not inside the body. Just for show. Just
for the parties & the traveling alone. A few days pass, the fog

has lifted. It threatens to rain but never does. I'm used to this.
What is made great in shadows does not always see the light.

I wonder if it's harmful to consistently dream.
& not to stretch the math of clouds to its limit.

WHAT IT FEELS LIKE AT THE END

& when I saw the lamb

I thought:

how funny it is that three years
have passed.

Sky like a parapet,

open

I feel more powerful than ever.
Feel more like

a great earthquake

I am often held together
by others. What they say

& how they say it.

Want to make dinner
for my mother. & my love.

& the sun became black like sackcloth

I drank a beer or two with a boy with
glasses. He stared at me. & I thought
about whether or not this would end

with sex. Maybe this time it wouldn't.
We'd be two loaves of bread
staring at each other in a dark kitchen.

& the whole moon turned blood red

I seem to fall madly in love
with every boy I touch. Midas.
It's a curse. The second boy

whose father is dead. The pulse
of masculinity. Rips through
us, violent waves.

I left him
with my lips.

& the stars of the sky fell to earth

WHEN YOU ARE READY TO LOVE AGAIN

History is simple. Something happened here. & then
it is gone. Your blue dress from Tuesday is now a dish

rag. You're contemplating the storm.
Here's a present, sweet. A new stone.

I picked it up for you from near where the lake becomes
a river. I would have gone in the water & grabbed you a

fish with my bare hands. But the water always makes me
too docile, a soft cooing babe. So I have nothing really

good for you. Even my head is empty. The succulent on
my desk is dying. I've watered it several times this week.

Suddenly, your pursed lips. Ready for a kiss. When I lean
into them, you're gone like valley fog in midday, hard to

catch with the eye. I understand why the magpie sings
outside the window like a memory, historic. Because I'm

always affected by even the tiniest movement of a leaf.
I'm jarred open. I'm all the whispering to the wind.

PSALMS

I.

In my present state, the door to the room cracked,
the light spilling in, many years passed, I'm thinking

of your face. The bloom of daffodils that is your ears.
You have left us & now are breathing heaven.

II.

Remember, David, remember. Our song you played
in Bethlehem. Play that song again, we both remember.

David, you are to beat Goliath. It's written.
In a field, swollen with green, I'm your maiden.

III.

I'm damaged. David. There will be nothing
but this scent. The ambrosia. God is healthy.

Just like you, David. Your clear brown skin
in the desert light. They never told our story.

IV.

The last time when I took you to a cliff. Your hands claimed some rocks. This is what you taught me. Though you were

unaware: *hold onto something hard & real*. You are not aware of your hands. You never were. Where are your hands now?

Are you holding on to the light, David? Like the light that fills this hollow room? I'm cursed to the touch of you. In the shower.

Along the dry sidewalk to work. You unbutton me every chance that you get. & I like it, David. The small bump of your knuckles

against my chest.

V.

The spray of water near the sea. David.
You loved me against the wet sand.

VI.

I don't like men anymore. Thank God, David. Thank you for

foreshadowing some greater man. Your headstone now resting in Jerusalem. David, don't you remember your nails down

my back. Or my heart skipping a beat when you'd look at me like I had purposefully broken the glass. I won't be in here

forever, David. Soon I'll say *thy love to me was wonderful.*

travis tate is a queer, black playwright, poet and performer from Austin, Texas. Their poetry has appeared in *Borderlands:Texas Poetry Review, Underblong, Mr.Ma'am, apt,* and *Cosmonaut Avenue,* among other journals. They earned an MFA from the Michener Center for Writers. You can find more about them at **travisltate.com**.

www.ingramcontent.com/pod-product-compliance
Lightning Source LLC
Chambersburg PA
CBHW030350100526
44592CB00010B/897